D1370144

For Richard

Designed by Herman Lelie

Produced by Mathew Price Ltd
The Old Rectory House
Marston Magna
Yeovil
Somerset BA22 8DT
England

Canadian Cataloguing in Publication Data

Morozumi, Atsuko, 1955–
  One gorilla

ISBN 0-385-25255-2

I. Title.

PZ7.M6760n 1990   j823′.914   C90-093324-0

Published in Canada by
Doubleday Canada Limited,
105 Bond Street,
Toronto, Ontario
M5B 1Y3

Printed and bound in Hong Kong

ONE GORILLA

A Counting Book

Atsuko Morozumi

Doubleday Canada Limited, Toronto

Here is a list of things I love.
One gorilla.

Two butterflies among the flowers and one gorilla.

Three budgerigars in my house
and one gorilla.

Four squirrels in the woods
and one gorilla.

Five pandas in the snow
and one gorilla.

Six rabbits in a field
and one gorilla.

Seven frogs by the fence
and one gorilla.

Eight fish in the sea
and one gorilla.

Nine birds among the leaves
and one gorilla.

Ten cats in my garden
and one gorilla.

10 cats

9 birds

8 fish

7 frogs

6 rabbits

5 pandas

4 squirrels

3 budgerigars

2 butterflies

But where is my gorilla?

Ah, there he is.